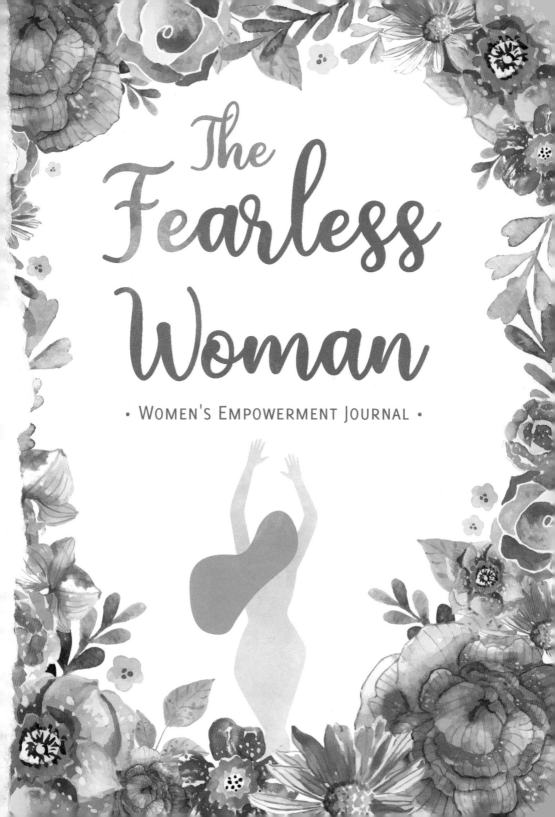

The Fearless Woman

· WOMEN'S EMPOWERMENT JOURNAL ·

Follow us on social media!

Tag us and use #piccadillyinc in your posts
for a chance to win monthly prizes!

10 9 8 7 6 5 4 3 2 1

Printed in China

ISBN-13: 978-1-62009-316-0

Introduction

Empowerment. It's a complete sentence, a verb, noun, and adjective. It's an emotion, movement, and it can be contagious. More importantly, empowerment is liberating. Freedom from limitations we put upon ourselves, freedom from bad habits and freedom from allowing others' negativity to disrupt our life. It is the total destruction of the prison we build around ourselves by our own negative thinking and self-sabotaging behavior.

Empowerment

Authority or power given to someone to do something. The process of becoming stronger and more confident, especially in controlling one's life and claiming one's rights.

Author Ayn Rand said it best when she said,

> **The question isn't who's going to let me; it's who is going to stop me.**

As you complete this journal, tap into your inner strength that already lies within. Allow this journey to inspire and enrich you with a strong sense of empowerment that you can share with the world. Be bold, be brave, but most of all, be yourself.

Internal Empowerment

This section will help you determine how much you empower yourself.

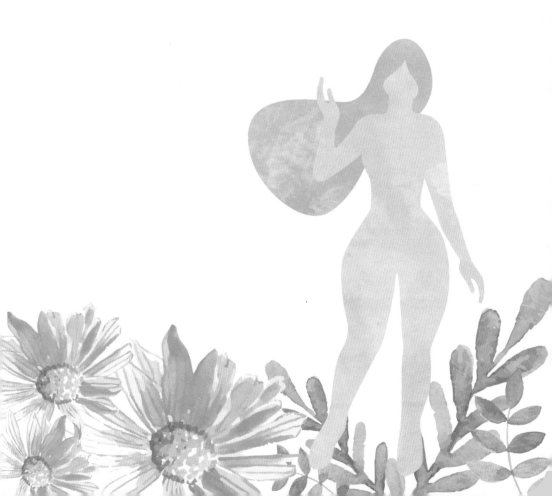

Internal Empowerment

1. Are you self-motivating? How easy is it to motivate yourself and what is the hardest thing about trying to stay motivated? What can you do to better motivate yourself?

_____

_____

_____

_____

_____

_____

_____

_____

2. What kind of thoughts occupy your mind? Are they mostly positive, negative, or a mixture of both? How can you improve the quality of your thoughts, so that they start empowering you?

_____

_____

_____

_____

_____

_____

_____

_____

_____

_____

I empower myself.

3. What makes you feel empowered? Is it a song, an activity, book, or movie? How can you incorporate empowering things into your daily routine?

_____

_____

_____

_____

_____

_____

_____

_____

4. How is your confidence level? What boosts your confidence and what additional steps can you take to sustain your confidence?

_____

_____

_____

_____

_____

_____

_____

_____

_____

_____

_____

> " I dwell in possibility. "
>
> -Emily Dickinson

Internal Empowerment

5. What makes you feel strong? How often do you do things that make you feel strong? What have you been wanting to do, that you feel will empower strength within?

_____

_____

_____

_____

_____

_____

_____

_____

6. Do you surround yourself with positive people or negative people? What can you do to create a more positive and empowering circle of support in your life?

_____

_____

_____

_____

_____

_____

_____

_____

_____

> " We must believe that we are gifted for something, and that this thing, at whatever cost, must be attained. "
>
> -Marie Curie

I empower myself.

7. What drains your energy and doesn't impact your life positively? Have you thought about making a change, and if not, why?

_____
_____
_____
_____
_____
_____
_____
_____
_____

8. Are you avoiding anything or anyone? Do you have any unresolved conflicts or fears you need to face? If so, make a plan to confront them in a positive manner and how you think this will empower you.

_____
_____
_____
_____
_____
_____
_____
_____
_____
_____
_____

Internal Empowerment

9. Are you wearing a mask? Do you feel you're pretending to be something you're not to please someone else? What can you do to be your most authentic self?

_____
_____
_____
_____
_____
_____
_____
_____

10. Are you lying to yourself about anything? Have you evaluated unresolved internal conflicts? What do you need to have an honest conversation with yourself about?

_____
_____
_____
_____
_____
_____
_____
_____
_____
_____
_____

I empower myself.

11. Do you continually challenge yourself, if so, how? What additional ways can you add empowering challenges or goals to your life?

_____
_____
_____
_____
_____
_____
_____
_____

12. Have you created a vision board for your life, and if so, what's on it and why? If you haven't, what could you put on the board that will empower and fuel your inner champion?

_____
_____
_____
_____
_____
_____
_____
_____

> " Virtue can only flourish
> amongst equals... "
>
> -Mary Wollstonecraft

Internal Empowerment

13. Do you encourage yourself enough? Write about ways you can encourage and pamper yourself when you need an extra dose of self-love?

_____

_____

_____

_____

_____

_____

_____

_____

14. Do you sabotage yourself sometimes, and if so, how? What can you do to change this behavior? Why do you think you do this?

_____

_____

_____

_____

_____

_____

_____

_____

_____

> " Whenever I hear a man talking of the advantages of our ill-used sex, I look upon it as the prelude to some new act of authority. "
>
> -Letitia Elizabeth Landon

I empower myself.

15. Have you thought about the connection between your physical and mental health? What physical activities do you enjoy that can boost your positive mental health?

_____

_____

_____

_____

_____

_____

_____

_____

_____

16. How easy do you set and accomplish your goals? Have you evaluated how much you've achieved and if you're encountering any roadblocks that could be removed through a new sense of empowerment?

_____

_____

_____

_____

_____

_____

_____

_____

_____

_____

_____

Internal Empowerment

17. What ways can you feed your inner strength? Do you practice affirmations, why or why not?

_____
_____
_____
_____
_____
_____
_____
_____

18. How do you deal with failure or setbacks? What can you do differently to always gain something positive from them?

_____
_____
_____
_____
_____
_____
_____
_____
_____
_____
_____

19. Are you stretching yourself too thin or allowing yourself to become too stressed? What areas of your life could use a makeover?

_____

_____

_____

_____

_____

_____

_____

_____

_____

20. What do you feel are your weaknesses? Can you derive strength through them in any way?

_____

_____

_____

_____

_____

_____

_____

_____

_____

_____

_____

" The best protection any woman
can have... is courage. "
-Elizabeth Cady Stanton

External Empowerment

This section will help you determine how much you empower others.

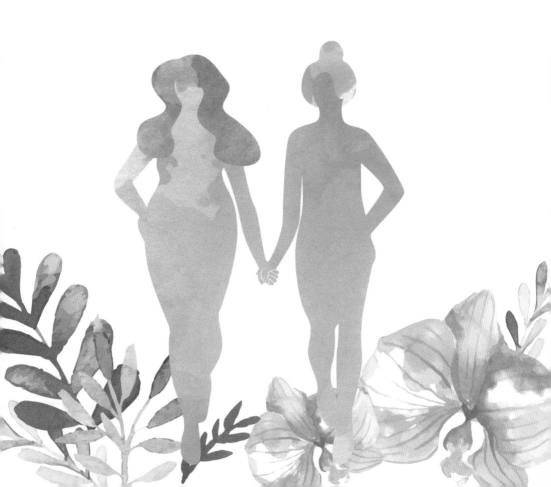

External Empowerment

1. How good are you at motivating others and what do you usually do to get people motivated?

_____
_____
_____
_____
_____
_____
_____
_____

2. Do you edify other people and speak positively to them, or do you tear others down harshly? What would people say about how you treat others?

_____
_____
_____
_____
_____
_____
_____
_____
_____
_____

3. Do you encourage others? Do you help others achieve their goals or lift their spirits when they have a bad day?

_____
_____
_____
_____
_____
_____
_____
_____
_____

4. What kind of example do you set to people around you and do you need to improve in any area here?

_____
_____
_____
_____
_____
_____
_____
_____
_____

> **No one can make you feel inferior without your consent.**
>
> -Eleanor Roosevelt

External Empowerment

5. Do you hold grudges or harbor resentment? Is there anyone in your life you need to forgive (remember forgiveness is freedom for you) or an apology you owe someone?

_____

_____

_____

_____

_____

_____

_____

6. Are you a person of integrity? Do you keep promises you make and do you apologize when you're wrong, why or why not? Do you need to improve here?

_____

_____

_____

_____

_____

_____

_____

> " Equality is the soul of liberty;
> there is, in fact, no liberty without it. "
>
> -Frances Wright

I empower others.

7. Have you ever felt like a doormat for someone else or felt like you were being used, can you explain? What can you do to prevent this from happening?

_____

_____

_____

_____

_____

_____

_____

_____

_____

8. Are you an effective communicator? Do you express yourself honestly to others and do you communicate your emotions in a healthy manner? How do you feel about communication?

_____

_____

_____

_____

_____

_____

_____

_____

External Empowerment

9. Do you lead by example, if so, how?

_____
_____
_____
_____
_____
_____
_____
_____
_____

10. Do you have an outlet like a blog, vlog or platform you can empower others through? If not, what would you like to start doing to motivate others positively?

_____
_____
_____
_____
_____
_____
_____
_____
_____
_____
_____
_____

11. Are you a good support system for someone else? How dependable are you when others you care about are in need?

_____
_____
_____
_____
_____
_____
_____
_____
_____

12. How positive is your social media presence? Are you negative in public forums, do you argue, or do you use these opportunities as a way to empower? What could you do better?

_____
_____
_____
_____
_____
_____
_____
_____

> The best and most beautiful things in the world cannot be seen nor even touched, but just felt in the heart.
>
> -Helen Keller

External Empowerment

13. What kind of listener are you? Do you always try and speak, or do you generally try and learn by listening to others? How much do you value learning from other people?

_____
_____
_____
_____
_____
_____
_____
_____

14. Has pride ever gotten in the way of a friendship or relationship? What happened and what would you do differently now?

_____
_____
_____
_____
_____
_____
_____
_____

> " Life is not what it's supposed to be.
> It's what it is. The way you cope with it
> is what makes the difference. "
>
> -Virginia Satir

15. Do you hurt others when you're having a bad day? What can you do to change this behavior moving forward?

_____

_____

_____

_____

_____

_____

_____

_____

_____

16. Have you ever helped someone right a wrong or fight for injustice, if so, how? If not, how can you give back in this empowering area?

_____

_____

_____

_____

_____

_____

_____

_____

_____

_____

External Empowerment

17. Who is the most empowering person you've ever met and how were they empowering? Did you share their energy of empowerment with others?

_____

_____

_____

_____

_____

_____

_____

_____

18. Do you have healthy work relationships with others? What can you do better to foster a more empowering work dynamic? Are you a team player?

_____

_____

_____

_____

_____

_____

_____

_____

_____

_____

I empower others.

19. Do you criticize other people or yourself too much? How do you feel when others criticize you?

_____
_____
_____
_____
_____
_____
_____
_____
_____

20. Do you make friends easily and get along with others? How do you act when you meet new people?

_____
_____
_____
_____
_____
_____
_____
_____
_____
_____

> **" I would rather die of passion than of boredom. "**
> -Émile Zola

Environmental Empowerment

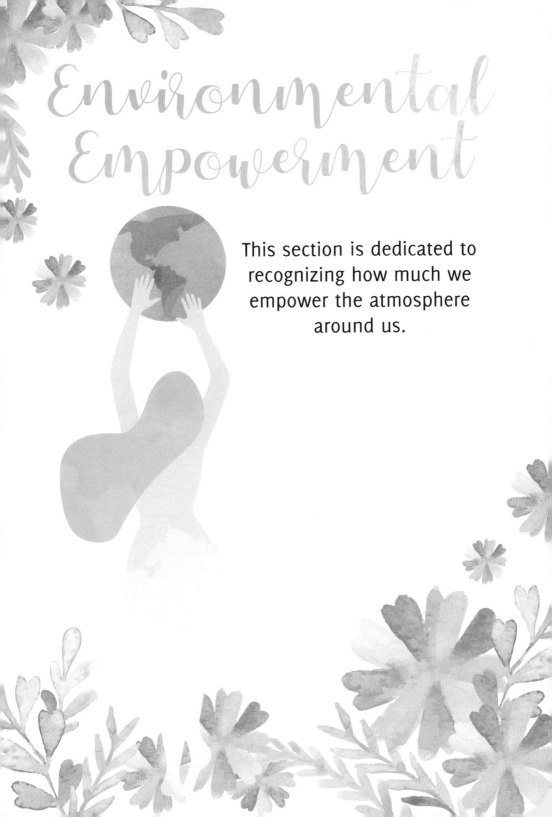

This section is dedicated to recognizing how much we empower the atmosphere around us.

Environmental Empowerment

1. Do you interact with positive leaders, mentors, and influencers? How can you get more involved with people that will empower you?

_____

_____

_____

_____

_____

_____

_____

2. How do you lend a helping hand and what specific area would you like to help more with?

_____

_____

_____

_____

_____

_____

_____

_____

_____

_____

I empower the atmosphere around me.

3. What opportunities for change would you like to create or get involved with?

_____
_____
_____
_____
_____
_____
_____
_____
_____

4. What have you found that you're passionate about and how do you contribute or how would you like to start contributing?

_____
_____
_____
_____
_____
_____
_____
_____
_____

> " What a wonderful life I've had!
> I only wish I'd
> realized it sooner. "
>
> –Colette

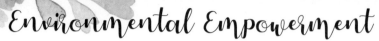

5. Are you involved in an empowering group or movement? If so, what, and if not, what empowering group would you like to join and why?

_____

_____

_____

_____

_____

_____

_____

_____

6. In what ways can you give back or improve the community around you?

_____

_____

_____

_____

_____

_____

_____

_____

> " I wouldn't sweat too much what it is,
> where it is or what you're doing,
> as long as you're learning. "
>
> -Melanie Whelan

I empower the atmosphere around me.

7. Who would you love to meet that you feel you could learn from and would empower you the most and why?

_____
_____
_____
_____
_____
_____
_____
_____

8. What is the biggest struggle in your community and why? How do you feel about this?

_____
_____
_____
_____
_____
_____
_____
_____
_____
_____
_____

Environmental Empowerment

9. Do you have an unresolved conflict with family or friends that you've been avoiding? Why haven't you resolved this yet and how can you?

_____

_____

_____

_____

_____

_____

_____

10. In what ways can you start empowering your immediate circle of friends and family?

_____

_____

_____

_____

_____

_____

_____

_____

_____

_____

I empower the atmosphere around me.

11. Where is your favorite place to visit that gives you a sense of empowerment and why does it make you feel this way?

_____

_____

_____

_____

_____

_____

_____

12. What is the one thing you think you need to change most about your current situation and why?

_____

_____

_____

_____

_____

_____

_____

_____

> " There never will be complete equality until women themselves help to make laws and elect lawmakers. "
>
> -Susan B. Anthony

Environmental Empowerment

13. What do you think is the most constructive use of your time?

_____

_____

_____

_____

_____

_____

_____

14. If you think globally, what changes would you like to see in the next 10 years and how do you think you can contribute to that change?

_____

_____

_____

_____

_____

_____

_____

> **There is a woman at the beginning of all great things.**
>
> -Alphonse de Lamartine

I empower the atmosphere around me.

15. What makes you feel overwhelmed and why? How can you take small steps to turn that feeling of being overwhelmed into empowerment?

_____

_____

_____

_____

_____

_____

_____

_____

16. Do you feel helpless about any specific topic, cause, or problem, and if so, why? How can you shed a positive light on this issue?

_____

_____

_____

_____

_____

_____

_____

_____

_____

_____

_____

Environmental Empowerment

17. How important do you think it is to have a positive outlook? Describe your outlook on life.

_____

_____

_____

_____

_____

_____

_____

18. Brainstorm some exciting and empowering goals for places or people in need and write about how you can empower those in your community to help.

_____

_____

_____

_____

_____

_____

_____

_____

_____

_____

19. What global charity or mission do you feel close to and how can you help contribute more to the cause?

_____

_____

_____

_____

_____

_____

_____

_____

20. Have you ever paid it forward, and if so, how? Doing good things for others, being honest, and kind gestures are great ways to pay it forward. Has someone paid it forward to you?

_____

_____

_____

_____

_____

_____

_____

> **"** Know why you believe, understand what you believe, and possess a reason for the faith that is in you. **"**
>
> -Frances Wright

Empowerment Interference

This section will help you recognize what hinders you from feeling empowered.

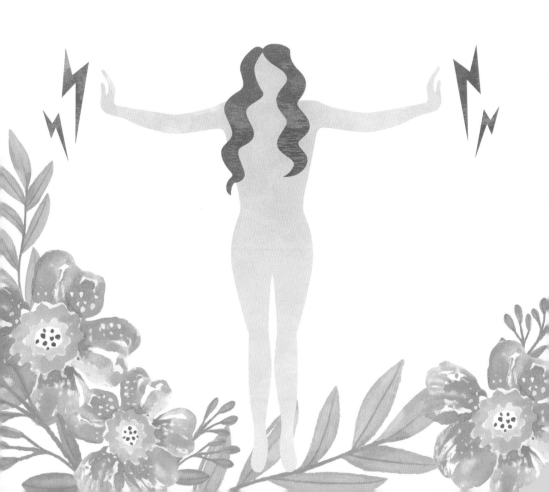

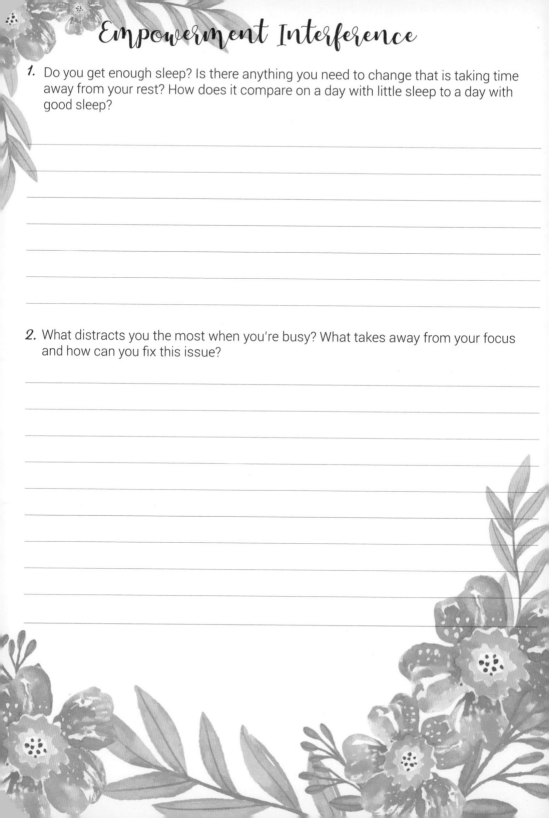

Empowerment Interference

1. Do you get enough sleep? Is there anything you need to change that is taking time away from your rest? How does it compare on a day with little sleep to a day with good sleep?

_____

_____

_____

_____

_____

_____

_____

2. What distracts you the most when you're busy? What takes away from your focus and how can you fix this issue?

_____

_____

_____

_____

_____

_____

_____

_____

_____

_____

_____

I recognize what keeps me from feeling empowered.

3. Does anything or anyone make you feel weak, if so, what/who and why? Formulate a plan immediately below to remedy this situation for your journey towards empowerment.

_____

_____

_____

_____

_____

_____

_____

4. Do you make excuses for yourself instead of taking responsibility? How can you become more accountable?

_____

_____

_____

_____

_____

_____

_____

_____

_____

" Life shrinks or expands
in proportion to one's courage. "

-Anaïs Nin

Empowerment Interference

5. Do you honor your commitments? How can you separate the important commitments from unimportant ones and dedicate your time where it will be best utilized?

---

6. Do you say yes when you really want to say no? In what ways can you take back your power from feeling pressured to do things you don't want to do?

---

66 *Life isn't about waiting for the storm to pass...*
It's about learning to dance in the rain! 99

-Vivian Greene

I recognize what keeps me from feeling empowered.

7. What do you find yourself dreading the most? How can you make life changes to get out of this uncomfortable place?

_____
_____
_____
_____
_____
_____
_____
_____
_____
_____

8. What makes you laugh? How can you add more laughter to your life?

_____
_____
_____
_____
_____
_____
_____
_____
_____

Empowerment Interference

9. Do you ever feel you're not good enough? Write an affirmation to yourself below that reminds you of all your great qualities and that you are enough.

_____

_____

_____

_____

_____

_____

_____

_____

10. Are you happy with the goals and dreams you've placed in your life? Do you need to reevaluate your journey? Has something changed and are you on the right path for your happiness?

_____

_____

_____

_____

_____

_____

_____

_____

_____

_____

I recognize what keeps me from feeling empowered.

11. How do you feel about work or school right now? Are you doing what you want to be doing or what you feel you have to do? Do you need to make a change?

_____

_____

_____

_____

_____

_____

_____

_____

_____

12. What book have you read that made you feel strong and inspired? What did you like about it? Go back and read it again.

_____

_____

_____

_____

_____

_____

_____

_____

> " I try to avoid looking forward or backward, and try to keep looking upward. "
>
> -Charlotte Brontë

Empowerment Interference

13. Is there a negative relationship or person you need to part company with? What are they doing to hinder your empowerment?

_____

_____

_____

_____

_____

_____

_____

_____

14. Do you procrastinate, and if so, what kind of procrastination are you doing? How can you fix this bad habit and improve your productivity?

_____

_____

_____

_____

_____

_____

_____

_____

_____

> " I'm not afraid of storms,
> for I'm learning how to sail my ship. "
>
> -Louisa May Alcott

I recognize what keeps me from feeling empowered.

15. What negative personality traits do you think hinder you and what positive personality traits help you excel? How can you improve here?

_____

_____

_____

_____

_____

_____

_____

_____

_____

_____

16. How well do you accept change? Do you think change is good or bad and what was the hardest change you ever made that had the most positive impact? How can you acclimate better to change?

_____

_____

_____

_____

_____

_____

_____

_____

_____

_____

Empowerment Interference

17. Do you set unrealistic expectations or goals that are impossible for yourself? How can you adjust your expectations to become more realistic?

_____

_____

_____

_____

_____

_____

_____

_____

18. Do you give up too easily? Why do you think this happens and what can you do to improve this area of your life?

_____

_____

_____

_____

_____

_____

_____

_____

_____

_____

_____

I recognize what keeps me from feeling empowered.

19. Do you let the opinions of those around you negatively impact you? How can you address this issue to create a more empowering outcome for all parties?

_____
_____
_____
_____
_____
_____
_____
_____

20. Are you angry about something, if so, what? How can you channel this anger in a positive way and use it as motivation?

_____
_____
_____
_____
_____
_____
_____

> " It is justice, not charity,
> that is wanting in the world. "
> -Mary Wollstonecraft

Celebrate Empowerment

Learning to appreciate others
and allowing ourselves to be empowered.

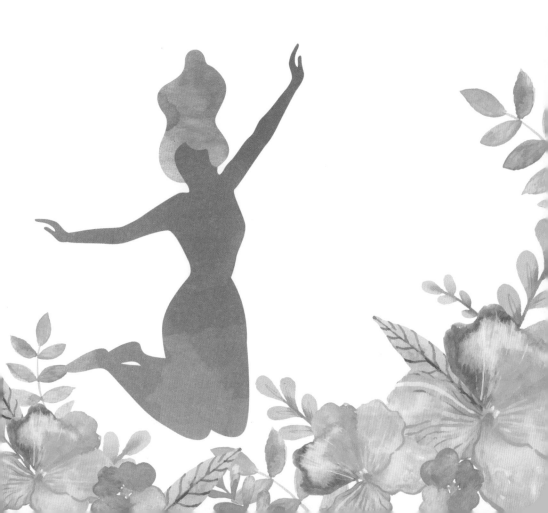

Celebrate Empowerment

1. Do you get jealous of other people's success or do you celebrate their accomplishments? Do you find that you compare yourself to others and it creates resentment and a negative pattern of thinking? What do you need to change?

_____

_____

_____

_____

_____

_____

_____

2. Who or what inspires you and why? How can you incorporate more of this inspiration into your daily life?

_____

_____

_____

_____

_____

_____

_____

_____

_____

_____

I appreciate others and allow myself to be empowered.

3. Do you share your passions or things that inspire you with others? Do you ask others what inspires them?

_____

_____

_____

_____

_____

_____

_____

_____

4. Have you ever felt in competition with another person, if so, why? Did you create this on your own and have you addressed the source of this feeling? How can you find empowerment here?

_____

_____

_____

_____

_____

_____

_____

> " The past, the present and the future
> are really one: they are today. "
>
> -Harriet Beecher Stowe

Celebrate Empowerment

5. How well do you get along with others? Do you feel it's important to get along with other people that are not your friends or family?

_____

_____

_____

_____

_____

_____

_____

_____

6. Do you compliment other people on their attributes and do you accept compliments well? What compliments have you received lately? Do you need to work on recognizing others good qualities?

_____

_____

_____

_____

_____

_____

_____

> *I would have girls regard themselves not as adjectives but as nouns.*
> -Elizabeth Cady Stanton

I appreciate others and allow myself to be empowered.

7. What could the world use more of and why?

_____

_____

_____

_____

_____

_____

_____

_____

8. Who is your biggest champion and is always rooting for your success? How do they make you feel and how do you feel about them?

_____

_____

_____

_____

_____

_____

_____

_____

_____

_____

Celebrate Empowerment

9. What qualities in women do you find empowering?

_____
_____
_____
_____
_____
_____
_____

10. What women through history do you find most empowering and why?

_____
_____
_____
_____
_____
_____
_____
_____
_____

I appreciate others and allow myself to be empowered.

11. Have you ever seen someone on the street that inspired you? Perhaps, it was a random person you watched and something about them touched you? Explain.

_____
_____
_____
_____
_____
_____
_____
_____
_____
_____

12. In what ways can you strive to better empower the people you meet?

_____
_____
_____
_____
_____
_____
_____
_____

> " I declare to you that woman must not depend upon the protection of man, but must be taught to protect herself... "
>
> -Susan B. Anthony

Celebrate Empowerment

13. What do you like about the word empower and how does it make you feel?

_____
_____
_____
_____
_____
_____
_____
_____

14. Who is the strongest woman you know and what makes them strong? Do they contribute to your empowerment in any way?

_____
_____
_____
_____
_____
_____
_____
_____

> " But woman's grief is like a summer storm,
> Short as it violent is... "
>
> -Joanna Baillie

I appreciate others and allow myself to be empowered.

15. Have you ever overcome a difficult situation or period in your life? If so, what was it and how did you overcome it?

_____

_____

_____

_____

_____

_____

_____

_____

_____

16. What do your facial expressions say about you? How often do you smile and what feedback do you often hear about it?

_____

_____

_____

_____

_____

_____

_____

_____

_____

_____

_____

Celebrate Empowerment

17. Do you like to share ideas with other people around you or listen when they share ideas? Elaborate on this.

_____

_____

_____

_____

_____

_____

_____

_____

18. How can you encourage creativity in other people? What can you do differently to be more encouraging and empowering?

_____

_____

_____

_____

_____

_____

_____

_____

_____

_____

I appreciate others and allow myself to be empowered.

19. Do you allow others to challenge you and do you challenge other people? Why do you think it's important to challenge each other and how can you do it in a positive way?

_____

_____

_____

_____

_____

_____

_____

20. What nice things have you done for others are you most proud of and how can you build on them?

_____

_____

_____

_____

_____

_____

_____

_____

> " The truth is the kindest thing
> we can give folks in the end. "
>
> -Harriet Beecher Stowe

Exploring Empowerment

The true meaning of empowerment.

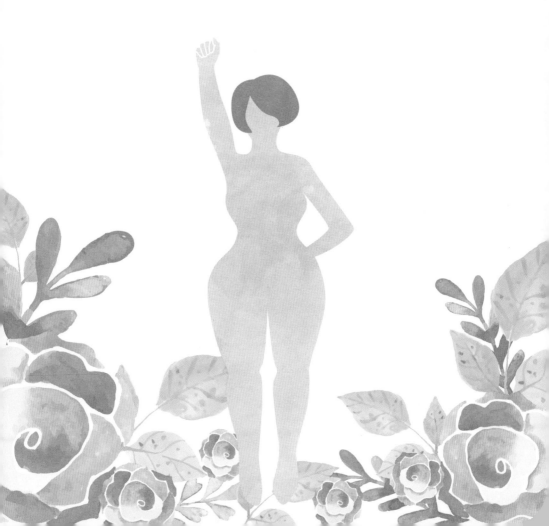

Exploring Empowerment

1. How empowered do you feel at this point in your life and is there anything you can do to improve the way you feel?

_____
_____
_____
_____
_____
_____
_____
_____

2. When you think of the word empower or empowerment, what comes to mind first? Are there any specific images you envision?

_____
_____
_____
_____
_____
_____
_____
_____
_____
_____

I know the true meaning of empowerment.

3. What have you learned about the word empowerment thus far through this journal?

_____
_____
_____
_____
_____
_____
_____
_____
_____
_____

4. What do you think is the most challenging obstacle on your way to achieving your strongest sense of empowerment?

_____
_____
_____
_____
_____
_____
_____
_____

> " Great difficulties may be surmounted
> by patience and perseverance. "
>
> -Abigail Smith Adams

Exploring Empowerment

5. How do you think becoming more empowered will improve your life for the better?

_____

_____

_____

_____

_____

_____

_____

_____

6. Do you think it's important to empower people around you, if so, why?

_____

_____

_____

_____

_____

_____

_____

_____

> " A woman only can understand a woman;
> and it is pleasant to be understood sometimes. "
>
> -Letitia Elizabeth Landon

I know the true meaning of empowerment.

7. Why do you think certain people in this world prevent others from becoming empowered?

_____
_____
_____
_____
_____
_____
_____
_____
_____

8. Do you appreciate diversity, other cultures, and differences in people? How do you think people can better celebrate each others' differences?

_____
_____
_____
_____
_____
_____
_____
_____
_____
_____

Exploring Empowerment

9. How big of a role do you think success or money plays in one's own sense of empowerment? Describe how you can feel empowered when you don't feel successful.

_____

_____

_____

_____

_____

_____

_____

_____

10. What are you doing right now to further your personal growth? What do you need to do?

_____

_____

_____

_____

_____

_____

_____

_____

_____

_____

I know the true meaning of empowerment.

11. Do you feel in control of your emotions or are you still a work in progress, can you explain? Also, how self-aware are you and what impact is this playing on your ability to feel empowered?

_____
_____
_____
_____
_____
_____
_____

12. What life lessons have you learned the most from and what did you learn?

_____
_____
_____
_____
_____
_____
_____

> " Life is either
> a daring adventure, or nothing. "
> -Helen Keller

Exploring Empowerment

13. Knowledge is power, and power is a strong component of empowerment. How are you continually learning? What is your main source of knowledge?

_____

_____

_____

_____

_____

_____

_____

14. Have you set standards for yourself, if so, what are they? How do you share your values with others, so they know areas where you won't compromise your character?

_____

_____

_____

_____

_____

_____

_____

> " And, of course, men know best about everything, except what women know better. "
>
> -George Eliot

I know the true meaning of empowerment.

15. Have you defined your own identity, and if so, can you describe it in a few words? Do you make your individuality clear to others, so they don't try and conform you?

_____

_____

_____

_____

_____

_____

_____

_____

16. Do you pay attention to your word choices and if your language is more positive or negative? How can you incorporate a more positive language in your daily life?

_____

_____

_____

_____

_____

_____

_____

_____

_____

_____

Exploring Empowerment

17. Are you closed-minded to others, and if so, how? What ways can you improve your open-mindedness without compromising your values or integrity?

_____

_____

_____

_____

_____

_____

_____

18. Do you value physical appearances more than personality and intelligence? Do you think empowerment comes from a physical or a more internal place and why?

_____

_____

_____

_____

_____

_____

_____

_____

_____

_____

_____

I know the true meaning of empowerment.

19. What oppressions from the past and present hinder most women from feeling empowered? What one thing in society must be changed and why?

_____

_____

_____

_____

_____

_____

_____

_____

_____

20. How is your commitment level to your health, goals, and overall sense of empowerment? Does anything interfere with your level of commitment?

_____

_____

_____

_____

_____

_____

_____

> 66 I am not afraid;
> I was born to do this. 99
>
> -Joan of Arc

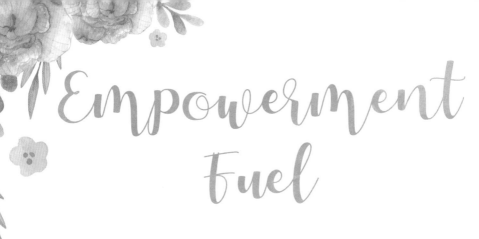

Empowerment Fuel

Learning what fuels your sense
of empowerment.

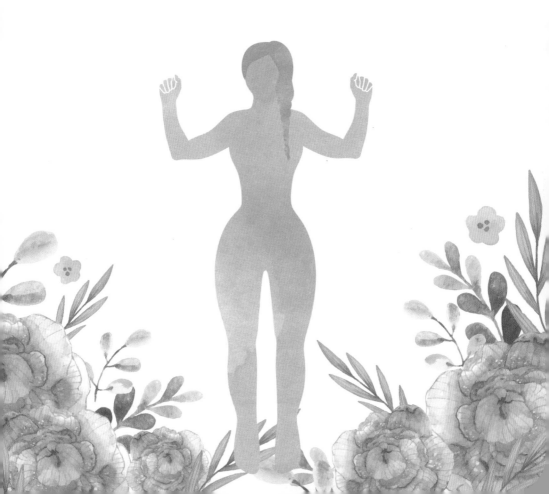

Empowerment Fuel

1. Describe a time you felt strong and empowered and what made you feel this way.

_____

_____

_____

_____

_____

_____

_____

_____

2. What are the different ways you can empower someone or be empowered yourself?

_____

_____

_____

_____

_____

_____

_____

_____

_____

_____

_____

_____

I know what fuels my sense of empowerment.

3. What activity always gives you a strong sense of empowerment?

_____
_____
_____
_____
_____
_____
_____
_____

4. What is the most empowering book you've ever read? What kind of goals can you set to read more inspirational books and what is the next book you want to read and why?

_____
_____
_____
_____
_____
_____

> ❝ Just as women's bodies
> are softer than men's,
> so their understanding is sharper. ❞
>
> -Christine de Pizan

Empowerment Fuel

5. What movie stirs up internal empowerment and why? How can you draw from this when you need extra strength?

_____

_____

_____

_____

_____

_____

_____

6. Do you have an empowerment song playlist, if so, what are a few of the songs on it? What other kinds of things can you curate to help you fuel your empowerment?

_____

_____

_____

_____

_____

_____

_____

_____

> *I am a free human being with an independent will, which I now exert to leave you.*
>
> -Charlotte Brontë

I know what fuels my sense of empowerment.

7. Have you ever experienced an emotional release, if so, can you describe it? What ways can you help yourself in this area to let go of negative emotions you have stored up?

8. Do you dwell on past mistakes, and if so, how does that make you feel? How can you learn from your mistakes and move on? What can you do to turn what you learned into fuel?

Empowerment Fuel

9. How courageous are you? Do you think you need to work on courage at any level to feel more empowered?

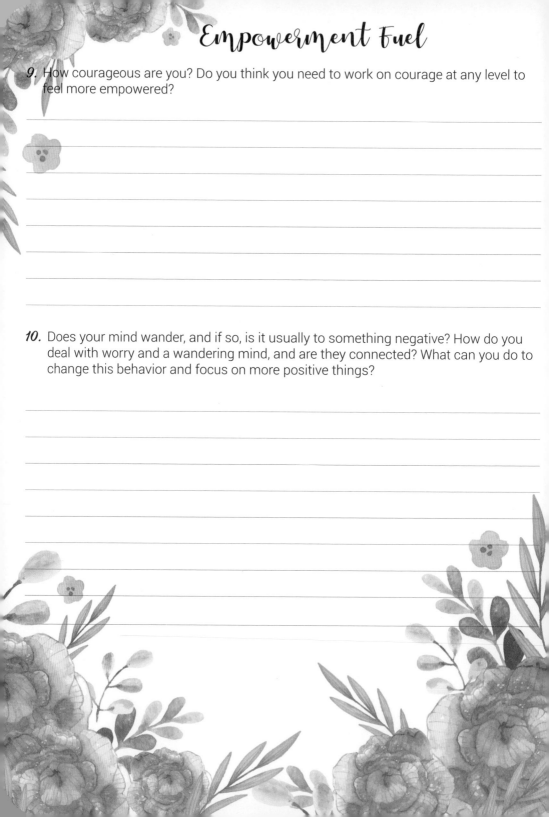

10. Does your mind wander, and if so, is it usually to something negative? How do you deal with worry and a wandering mind, and are they connected? What can you do to change this behavior and focus on more positive things?

I know what fuels my sense of empowerment.

11. How humble are you and how do you practice humility?

_____

_____

_____

_____

_____

_____

_____

_____

12. Have you ever joined a self-help group online or in person? What do you think of these and do you find them a good source of empowerment? Would you join?

_____

_____

_____

_____

_____

_____

_____

> *A lady's imagination is very rapid;*
> *it jumps from admiration to love,*
> *from love to matrimony in a moment.*
>
> -Jane Austen

Empowerment Fuel

13. How do you feel about gender equality right now? What needs to be improved and how can you promote change, so you feel empowered?

_____

_____

_____

_____

_____

_____

_____

14. How independent are you? What things do you do that give you a sense of independence and what are you working towards to become even more independent?

_____

_____

_____

_____

_____

_____

_____

> " I do not wish them [women]
> to have power over men;
> but over themselves. "
>
> -Mary Wollstonecraft

I know what fuels my sense of empowerment.

15. In what ways are you vulnerable and how do you handle knowing this? How can you celebrate these vulnerabilities so they become empowering?

16. In your opinion, what words are synonymous with empowerment and how can you start incorporating them into your vocabulary more?

Empowerment Fuel

17. Are you saving towards your future dreams and goals? Do you think having money saved gives you a sense of stability or empowerment? Can you have one without the other?

_____

_____

_____

_____

_____

_____

_____

18. How healthy is your self-esteem? What do you struggle with and what can you do to improve your self-esteem?

_____

_____

_____

_____

_____

_____

_____

_____

_____

_____

I know what fuels my sense of empowerment.

19. Do you have a sense of leadership in any area of your life? In what ways would you be a good leader and what leadership qualities do you have?

_____

_____

_____

_____

_____

_____

_____

_____

20. Have you been postponing something you really want to learn or something you want to do, if so, why? How do you think this will empower you?

_____

_____

_____

_____

_____

_____

_____

> **She had resolved never again to belong to another than herself.**
>
> -Kate Chopin

Maintaining Empowerment

How you can maintain a sense of empowerment even in the hardest times.

Maintaining Empowerment

1. Do you have a special happy place you like to go when you feel sad, stressed, or overwhelmed? If so, where is it, and if not, where could it be? What type of surroundings make you feel calm during chaos?

_____

_____

_____

_____

_____

_____

_____

2. Do you read self-help or spiritually uplifting books? What specific topics do you like to read about when you feel down? Create a reading plan for when you need an empowerment boost.

_____

_____

_____

_____

_____

_____

_____

_____

I can always maintain a sense of empowerment.

3. Have you practiced yoga or meditation, and if so, are they beneficial to you? If those are not for you, find a practice that agrees with your lifestyle and try it. What other types of relaxation techniques are you interested in?

_____

_____

_____

_____

_____

_____

4. Spend time with things that give you joy. Do you love animals, babies or the beach? If you had to make a list of the top 10 things that make you smile, what would be on that list?

_____

_____

_____

_____

_____

_____

_____

> " I do not wish to be a coward
> like the father of mankind,
> and throw the blame upon a woman. "
>
> -Ouida

5. Do you volunteer to help others in need? Sometimes helping others is a great way to get our mind off our own problems and giving back is a great source of empowerment. Where would you like to volunteer your time?

_____

_____

_____

_____

_____

_____

_____

6. How is your patience level? How can you incorporate more ways to practice patience?

_____

_____

_____

_____

_____

_____

_____

> " It is better to arm
> and strengthen your hero,
> than to disarm and enfeeble your foe. "
>
> -Anne Brontë

I can always maintain a sense of empowerment.

7. What activities do you love that help you keep a positive mindset? What new activities are you willing to try to help you feel less stressed?

_____

_____

_____

_____

_____

_____

_____

_____

_____

8. Do you have a friend or person that you can call when times get tough? Who do you like to confide in and do you allow anyone to confide in you?

_____

_____

_____

_____

_____

_____

_____

_____

_____

9. Writing is therapeutic, do you like to write? Do you write in a journal or have specific things you like to write when you need an outlet, can you explain?

_____
_____
_____
_____
_____
_____
_____
_____

10. Where is your favorite place to go for a walk? Do you make time to get away when you need to and if you had to pick a new route to explore, where would it be?

_____
_____
_____
_____
_____
_____
_____
_____

I can always maintain a sense of empowerment.

11. Do you allow yourself to be spoiled when you need a little TLC? What makes you feel better when times get hard and if you can't do your favorite thing, what are some other options?

_____

_____

_____

_____

_____

_____

_____

12. Do you sweat the small stuff, and if so, what small things do you allow to bother you that you probably shouldn't?

_____

_____

_____

_____

_____

_____

_____

> 66 Nothing is impossible,
> the word itself says I'm possible. 99
>
> -Audrey Hepburn

Maintaining Empowerment

13. How good are you at avoiding conflicts? Most of the time when we feel bad we take it out on others. In what ways can you avoid conflict and keep your peace?

_____

_____

_____

_____

_____

_____

_____

14. Can you spot the good in every situation? What are ways you can practice finding the silver lining and readjusting your focus?

_____

_____

_____

_____

_____

_____

_____

> " Are you a young lady?
> I am a thousand times better:
> I am an honest woman,
> and as such I will be treated. "
>
> -Charlotte Brontë

I can always maintain a sense of empowerment.

15. Do you have positive people in your life and do you spend enough time with them? What are some ways and where are some places you can find time to spend with more positive people?

_____

_____

_____

_____

_____

_____

_____

16. Are you spiritual and do you pray? How important is prayer in your life and does it help you in difficult times?

_____

_____

_____

_____

_____

_____

_____

_____

_____

17. Do you get easily offended or often take people out of context? What ways can you prevent or protect yourself from an offense? Do you think you're more sensitive during difficult times?

_____

_____

_____

_____

_____

_____

_____

18. Sometimes difficult periods in our lives are meant to teach us something. Have you ever learned anything from a difficult period in your life? What was it, and if not, what do you think you could learn about yourself during this time?

_____

_____

_____

_____

_____

_____

_____

I can always maintain a sense of empowerment.

19. In what ways are you a fighter, survivor, and champion?

_____

_____

_____

_____

_____

_____

_____

_____

20. What is the hardest thing you've ever had to endure to this point in your life and how did it make you a better person?

_____

_____

_____

_____

_____

_____

_____

> **" Every thought we think
> is creating our future. "**
>
> -Louise L. Hay

Encouraging Empowerment

How to help others feel empowered.

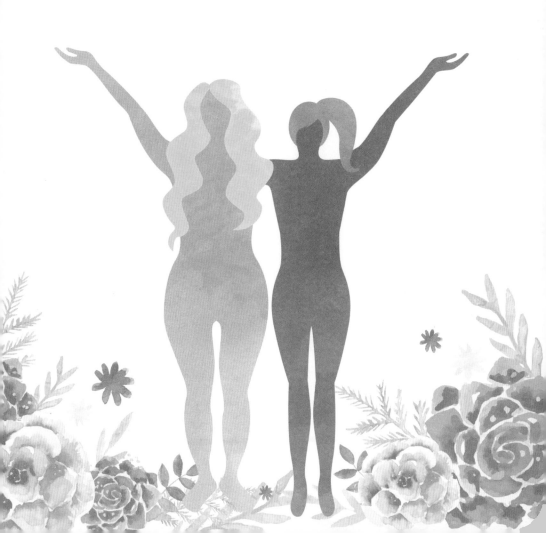

Encouraging Empowerment

1. Have you ever kicked others when they are down? In what ways can you provide encouragement to others when they feel low?

_____

_____

_____

_____

_____

_____

_____

2. Have you ever shared something you learned with someone else, if so, what was it? What things have you learned that would be empowering to share with others?

_____

_____

_____

_____

_____

_____

_____

_____

_____

I help others feel empowered.

3. Has anyone ever looked down on you, and if so, how did that make you feel? Have you done that to someone else? What can you do to make sure you identify, with other people in your life, in a positive way?

_____

_____

_____

_____

_____

_____

_____

4. Do you praise people when they do a good job? What specific relationships or areas of your life can you improve to be able to encourage the people around you?

_____

_____

_____

_____

_____

_____

_____

_____

> " I attribute my success to this:
> - I never gave or took any excuse. "
>
> -Florence Nightingale

Encouraging Empowerment

5. How kind are you to people, especially new people you meet? What things can you work on to become a kinder person? What are some examples of kindness?

_____

_____

_____

_____

_____

_____

_____

6. Do you participate in team building exercises and how do you feel about them? If you had to create your very own team building exercise, what would it be?

_____

_____

_____

_____

_____

_____

_____

> " You may be disappointed if you fail,
> but you are doomed
> if you don't try. "
>
> -Beverly Sills

I help others feel empowered.

7. How polite are you? Do you say please and thank you or do you take for granted others' kindness?

_____

_____

_____

_____

_____

_____

_____

_____

_____

8. Do you share or are you stingy with your possessions? Sharing is a great way to open up to someone and feel good doing it. What can you share more of?

_____

_____

_____

_____

_____

_____

_____

_____

_____

_____

Encouraging Empowerment

9. Have you ever judged a book by its cover and ended up being totally wrong, can you explain? How can you avoid doing this again?

_____

_____

_____

_____

_____

_____

_____

_____

10. What are specific ways that you can personally encourage and empower others?

_____

_____

_____

_____

_____

_____

_____

_____

_____

_____

_____

I help others feel empowered.

11. Is there an organization you've been wanting to get involved with that helps to empower others? What do they do and how do you feel you can help?

_____

_____

_____

_____

_____

_____

_____

_____

_____

12. Do you let people in your life know you appreciate them or is there room for improvement? Who in your life has done a lot of things for you and how have you expressed your appreciation for them?

_____

_____

_____

_____

_____

_____

_____

_____

> " Don't compromise yourself.
> You're all you've got. "
>
> -Janis Joplin

Encouraging Empowerment

13. Do you support a non-profit organization, if not, what organizations have you considered supporting and why? How will this be mutually beneficial for the empowerment process?

_____

_____

_____

_____

_____

_____

_____

14. Have you ever met someone that was super talented, and did you encourage their talents? How can you nurture talented people in your life?

_____

_____

_____

_____

_____

_____

_____

_____

> ❝ Your playing small
> does not serve the world. ❞
> -Marianne Williamson

15. What is your definition of thoughtfulness and how thoughtful are you? What are simple ways you can become a more thoughtful person?

_____

_____

_____

_____

_____

_____

_____

_____

_____

_____

16. Has anyone ever commented on your body language? How mindful are you of your body's actions when you talk and interact with people? What are some things you need to correct?

_____

_____

_____

_____

_____

_____

_____

_____

_____

_____

_____

Encouraging Empowerment

17. Are you introverted or extroverted? How can you empower someone who is the complete opposite of you?

_____

_____

_____

_____

_____

_____

_____

_____

18. Do you argue with others who have a different opinion than you? How can you be more open to discussions and less argumentative?

_____

_____

_____

_____

_____

_____

_____

_____

_____

_____

I help others feel empowered.

19. What is one thing you think everyone should do that would make them feel empowered?

_____

_____

_____

_____

_____

_____

_____

_____

_____

20. Do you treat others the way you want to be treated? Are you guilty of breaking that golden rule? If so, how and what can you do to improve?

_____

_____

_____

_____

_____

_____

_____

_____

_____

> **"** *But knowledge is the same for every mind, and every mind may and ought to be trained to receive it.* **"**
>
> -Frances Wright

Empowerment in Motion

Learning to put your sense of empowerment to good use.

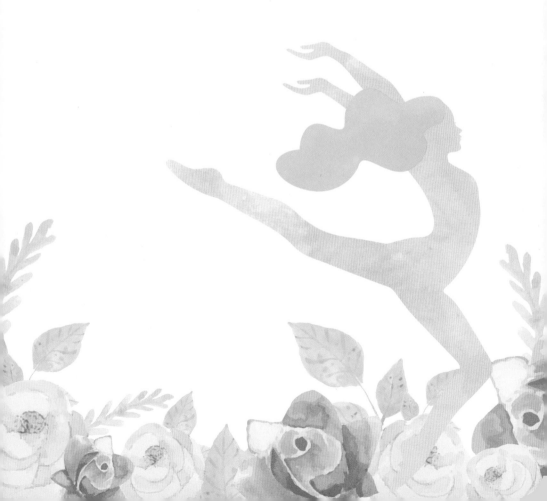

Empowerment in Motion

1. What are your fears or concerns about other women around the world and how can you aid in empowering them?

_____
_____
_____
_____
_____
_____
_____
_____

2. How do you encourage and empower the youth or younger generations of today? What challenges do they face that could hinder their sense of empowerment?

_____
_____
_____
_____
_____
_____
_____
_____
_____
_____

I put my sense of empowerment to good use.

3. Have you ever mentored anyone? What kind of mentor do you think you'd be and what would you love to mentor someone with?

_____

_____

_____

_____

_____

_____

_____

_____

4. What creative talents do you have that you could put to use to empower others?

_____

_____

_____

_____

_____

_____

_____

_____

_____

" Above all,
be the heroine in your life,
not the victim. "

-Nora Ephron

Empowerment in Motion

5. What specific point or story about your life could you share to encourage someone else in need of encouragement?

_____

_____

_____

_____

_____

_____

_____

_____

6. Do you have a heart that is willing to serve and help others? If so, how and why this particular area?

_____

_____

_____

_____

_____

_____

_____

_____

> " Never bend your head. Always hold it high.
> Look the world straight in the eye. "
>
> -Helen Keller

I put my sense of empowerment to good use.

7. Who do you think needs the most sense of empowerment right now? Is there any specific group or person?

_____

_____

_____

_____

_____

_____

_____

_____

8. Is there someone in your life that is having a hard time reaching their goal/s? If so, how can you empower them and help them get closer to victory?

_____

_____

_____

_____

_____

_____

_____

_____

_____

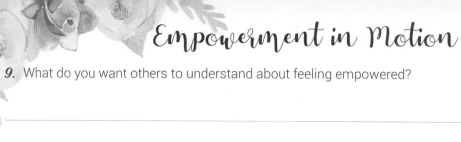

Empowerment in Motion

9. What do you want others to understand about feeling empowered?

_____

_____

_____

_____

_____

_____

_____

10. How can you empower people in your family?

_____

_____

_____

_____

_____

_____

_____

_____

_____

_____

_____

I put my sense of empowerment to good use.

11. How passionate are you about empowering others and what do you gain from helping others feel empowered?

_____

_____

_____

_____

_____

_____

_____

_____

12. Describe your community and specific organizations you care about and what empowering people through those channels will accomplish.

_____

_____

_____

_____

_____

_____

_____

" It took me quite a long time to develop a voice, and now that I have it, I am not going to be silent. "

-Madeleine Albright

Empowerment in Motion

13. What new things are you willing to try or learn to help empower others?

_____

_____

_____

_____

_____

_____

_____

_____

14. Who else can you get involved in helping empower others and what will they bring to the table?

_____

_____

_____

_____

_____

_____

_____

_____

_____

> " I have learned over the years that when one's mind is made up, this diminishes fear. "
>
> -Rosa Parks

I put my sense of empowerment to good use.

15. Have you contacted your local news about a cause or organization in your community you want to shed light on? What specific channels can you use to fuel your empowerment agenda?

_____

_____

_____

_____

_____

_____

_____

16. How can you encourage or empower others with negative mindsets? What tools will you use to help them?

_____

_____

_____

_____

_____

_____

_____

_____

_____

_____

_____

17. What things will you need to avoid in order to be successful on your journey towards empowering yourself and others?

_____

_____

_____

_____

_____

_____

_____

_____

18. Do you think you need to take any courses or classes on counseling or seek support to make you a more effective person who empowers?

_____

_____

_____

_____

_____

_____

_____

_____

_____

_____

_____

I put my sense of empowerment to good use.

19. What is the biggest need or situation you see where empowering a person will be a game changer for their life?

_____

_____

_____

_____

_____

_____

_____

20. What do you hope to accomplish through your journey of empowerment?

_____

_____

_____

_____

_____

_____

_____

> 66 Courage is like a muscle;
> we strengthen it with use. 99
> -Ruth Gordon

Discovery

The following 25 questions will require research and reflection on your part. They are prompts that will guide you to find sources and stories of empowerment to use moving forward in your life. They will serve as a resource you can tap into when you're in need of encouragement or you need to encourage others. You can use people you know or don't know for these prompts. For certain questions, you should research online or through books at your library about people who fit the writing prompt criteria.

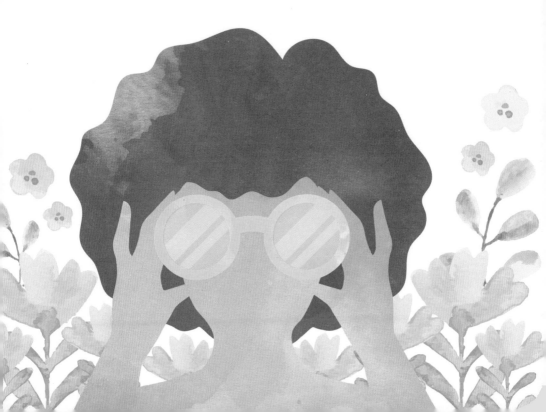

Discovery

1. Find a person who has a story of overcoming a disability. Write a brief summary of their story, how it inspired and empowered you. Be sure to include what you learned from them and what (if any) challenges you have in common.

_____

_____

_____

_____

_____

_____

_____

_____

_____

_____

_____

_____

_____

_____

_____

_____

_____

_____

_____

_____

_____

I am open to discovery.

2. Who in your family overcame a hardship that empowered you? What did they face, how did they overcome it, and why did it empower you?

_____

_____

_____

_____

_____

_____

_____

_____

_____

_____

_____

_____

_____

_____

_____

_____

_____

_____

_____

_____

_____

> ❝ The most difficult thing
> is the decision to act,
> the rest is merely tenacity. ❞
>
> -Amelia Earhart

Discovery

3. Find inspiring quotes about empowerment and strength and write your top 10 favorites below and who said them.

1.

2.

3.

4.

5.

6.

7.

8.

9.

10.

> 66 *You are imperfect,*
> *permanently and inevitably flawed.*
> *And you are beautiful.* 99
>
> -Amy Bloom

4. What movement in history was made that, in your opinion, would not have happened without a sense of empowerment?

_____

_____

_____

_____

_____

_____

_____

_____

_____

_____

_____

_____

_____

_____

_____

_____

_____

_____

_____

_____

_____

_____

_____

Discovery

5. Who is someone that has been in the news lately that has touched or empowered you and why?

_____

_____

_____

_____

_____

_____

_____

_____

_____

_____

_____

_____

_____

_____

_____

_____

_____

_____

_____

_____

_____

I am open to discovery.

6. What celebrity empowers you the most and why?

_____

_____

_____

_____

_____

_____

_____

_____

_____

_____

_____

_____

_____

_____

_____

_____

_____

_____

_____

_____

_____

_____

" *The most common way people give up their power is by thinking they don't have any.* "

-Alice Walker

Discovery

7. Pick a woman from history that made the biggest impact through empowerment and how she empowered others to achieve change.

66 *A woman's lot is made for her by the love she accepts.* 99

-George Eliot

8. Name someone who is no longer alive that you would have loved to meet because they were so inspiring. What is the one question you'd ask them?

_____

_____

_____

_____

_____

_____

_____

_____

_____

_____

_____

_____

_____

_____

_____

_____

_____

_____

_____

_____

_____

_____

Discovery

9. Name someone who is still living that you'd love to meet because they are so inspiring. What is the one question you'd ask them?

_____

_____

_____

_____

_____

_____

_____

_____

_____

_____

_____

_____

_____

_____

_____

_____

_____

_____

_____

_____

_____

_____

_____

10. What professions do you find inspiring and empowering, and why?

> " Women are never stronger
> than when they arm themselves
> in their weakness. "
>
> -Madame Marie du Deffand

Discovery

11. Name a famous lawyer, past or present, who changed history. How did that change empower you?

_____
_____
_____
_____
_____
_____
_____
_____
_____
_____
_____
_____
_____
_____
_____
_____
_____
_____
_____
_____
_____

> " Self-development is a higher duty
> than self-sacrifice. "
> -Elizabeth Cady Stanton

12. What part of the women's rights movement made you feel the most empowered?

_____

_____

_____

_____

_____

_____

_____

_____

_____

_____

_____

_____

_____

_____

_____

_____

_____

_____

_____

_____

_____

_____

_____

Discovery

13. What event from history can we learn from where someone tried to strip people of their empowerment?

I am open to discovery.

14. What activist is an example of true empowerment. How do you feel about them and what they stand for?

_____
_____
_____
_____
_____
_____
_____
_____
_____
_____
_____
_____
_____
_____
_____
_____
_____
_____
_____
_____

> " Courage is not the absence of fear,
> but rather the judgment that something else
> is more important than fear. "
>
> -Ambrose Redmoon

Discovery

15. What movements past or present make you feel empowered and why?

_____

_____

_____

_____

_____

_____

_____

_____

_____

_____

_____

_____

_____

_____

_____

_____

_____

_____

_____

> *Always be a first-rate version of yourself, instead of a second-rate version of somebody else.*
>
> -Judy Garland

I am open to discovery.

16. Who do you find heroic and what about them inspires you?

Discovery

17. Do you have someone local, within your community you admire? What do you like about them and how do they inspire or empower you?

18. What athlete, past or present, overcame adversity only to triumph? What happened and how does their story make you feel?

_____

_____

_____

_____

_____

_____

_____

_____

_____

_____

_____

_____

_____

_____

_____

_____

_____

_____

_____

_____

_____

> " *The most courageous act is still to think for yourself. Aloud.* "
>
> -Coco Chanel

Discovery

19. What political leader has inspired you? What specific cause or thing did they stand for that gave you a sense of empowerment?

_____

_____

_____

_____

_____

_____

_____

_____

_____

_____

_____

_____

_____

_____

_____

_____

_____

_____

_____

_____

> 66 *You must do the things you think you cannot do.* 99
>
> -Eleanor Roosevelt

I am open to discovery.

20. Do you know anyone who has dedicated their life to helping others? What did they do and what impact did that have on you? (It can be someone famous or not)

Discovery

21. What celebrity was an ambassador or representative for a worthy cause that inspired you and how did they make an impact in that organization?

_____
_____
_____
_____
_____
_____
_____
_____
_____
_____
_____
_____
_____
_____
_____
_____
_____
_____
_____
_____
_____
_____
_____

22. Have you ever been inspired or empowered by a philanthropist? If so, who, and how did they empower you through their good works?

_____
_____
_____
_____
_____
_____
_____
_____
_____
_____
_____
_____
_____
_____
_____
_____
_____
_____
_____
_____
_____

> 66 I can be changed by what happens to me,
> but I refuse to be reduced by it. 99
>
> -Maya Angelou

Discovery

23. What fictional story inspired or empowered you when you were younger? How do you feel about that story today?

_____

_____

_____

_____

_____

_____

_____

_____

_____

_____

_____

_____

_____

_____

_____

_____

_____

_____

_____

66 Women are the real
architects of society. 99

-Harriet Beecher Stowe

I am open to discovery.

24. What real-life biography did you find empowering and interesting? What separated this biography from so many others and how did it empower you?

_____

_____

_____

_____

_____

_____

_____

_____

_____

_____

_____

_____

25. What tragic natural disaster did you witness either in person or through the news that impacted you? What stories of empowerment emerged from the tragedies?

_____

_____

_____

_____

_____

_____

_____

_____

_____

Summary

This will be the conclusion of your empowerment journey. The following writing prompts will be a brief look back at what you've learned and what you hope to learn. We hope they provide a solid foundation to begin your journey to empowerment and empowering others.

> " And the purpose of life, after all,
> is to live it, to taste experience to the utmost,
> to reach out eagerly and without fear
> for newer and richer experience. "
>
> -Eleanor Roosevelt

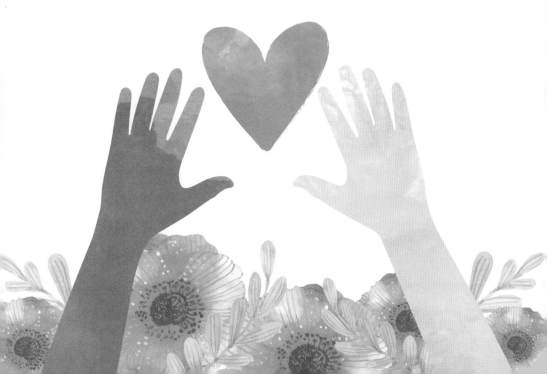

Summary

1. If you had to describe empowerment to someone, what would you say and what does empowerment look like to you?

_____

_____

_____

_____

_____

_____

_____

_____

_____

_____

_____

_____

_____

_____

_____

_____

_____

_____

_____

_____

_____

> " No man is good enough to govern any woman without her consent. "
>
> -Susan B. Anthony

I am on my journey to empowerment and empowering others.

2. What have you learned about yourself through this process?

_____

_____

_____

_____

_____

_____

_____

_____

_____

_____

_____

_____

_____

_____

_____

_____

_____

_____

_____

_____

_____

_____

_____

_____

Summary

3. What areas of your life would you like to focus on more to gain the sense of empowerment you desire?

_____

_____

_____

_____

_____

_____

_____

_____

_____

_____

_____

_____

_____

_____

_____

_____

_____

_____

_____

_____

_____

_____

_____

_____

_____

I am on my journey to empowerment and empowering others.

4. What changes do you feel you need to make to achieve a total sense of empowerment?

_____
_____
_____
_____
_____
_____
_____
_____
_____
_____
_____
_____
_____
_____
_____
_____
_____
_____
_____
_____
_____

> " *I don't intend to die till I've enjoyed my life.*
> *Everyone has a right to happiness*
> *and sooner or later I will have it.* "
>
> -Louisa May Alcott

Summary

5. Are you going to change anything about how you spend your time or where you invest your time?

_____

_____

_____

_____

_____

_____

_____

_____

_____

_____

_____

_____

_____

_____

_____

_____

_____

_____

> " A woman's life is her love;
> she does not begin to live until she begins to love. "
>
> -Florence Marryat

I am on my journey to empowerment and empowering others.

6. What type of impact do you think empowering others around you will make and what will be your first step to take towards this journey?

_____
_____
_____
_____
_____
_____
_____
_____
_____
_____
_____
_____
_____
_____
_____
_____
_____
_____
_____
_____
_____

Summary

7. How hard will it be for you to make some necessary changes and where will you start first?

_____

_____

_____

_____

_____

_____

_____

_____

_____

_____

_____

_____

_____

_____

_____

_____

_____

_____

_____

_____

_____

_____

_____

I am on my journey to empowerment and empowering others.

8. What are your top sources for encouragement and empowerment? Will you seek out more or new sources, if so, where?

_____

_____

_____

_____

_____

_____

_____

_____

_____

_____

_____

_____

_____

_____

_____

_____

_____

_____

_____

_____

_____

❝ *Men, their rights, and nothing more; women, their rights, and nothing less.* **❞**

-Susan B. Anthony

Summary

9. What do you want others to learn about you or from you that will help them on their journey of empowerment?

_____

_____

_____

_____

_____

_____

_____

_____

_____

_____

_____

_____

_____

_____

_____

_____

_____

_____

_____

_____

_____

> " When the sun is shining I can do anything;
> no mountain is too high,
> no trouble too difficult to overcome. "
>
> -Wilma Rudolph

I am on my journey to empowerment and empowering others.

10. What do you think are some of the keys to a healthy sense of empowerment?

_____
_____
_____
_____
_____
_____
_____
_____
_____
_____
_____
_____
_____
_____
_____
_____
_____
_____
_____
_____
_____
_____

Looking for more?

Similar titles available by Piccadilly:

300 Writing Prompts

300 MORE Writing Prompts

500 Writing Prompts

3000 Questions About Me

3000 Would You Rather Questions

Choose Your Own Journal

Your Father's Story

Your Mother's Story

The Story of My Life

Write the Poem

Write the Story

300 Drawing Prompts

500 Drawing Prompts

Calligraphy Made Easy

Comic Sketchbook

Sketching Made Easy

100 Life Challenges

Awesome Social Media Quizzes

Find the Cat

Find 2 Cats

Time Capsule Letters

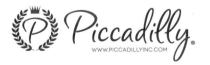